Introductory SQL

Quick Reference Guide

Comprehensive video training & instruction manuals available at www.teachucomp.com

TEACHUCOMP, INC.®
it's all about you

About Databases and SQL

Understanding Database Objects

A **table** is a collection of data about a certain subject: like customers, vendors or suppliers. It consists of *columns* and *rows* into which you store data.

A **field** is a *column* within a table. Fields all contain only one type of data. For example, within a customer table you might have a "First_Name" field into which you place only the customers' first names.

A **record** is a *row* within a table. A record contains one set of related field information about a single entry. For example, in a "Customer" table there may be a customer record that contains all of the field information about a single customer in a single row.

A **primary key** is a special relational database table column (or combination of columns) designated to uniquely identify each table record.

A **query** is used to extract only the data that you want or need to view from the tables. These objects are the "heart" of database design- and the whole point of using databases. Queries provide the data that is needed by the other database objects, often working in the background.

SQL is the language used to create the objects that exist within relational database management systems.

A **database** is the entire collection of tables, queries and other related objects.

A **relational database management system** (RDBMS) is software used to create and maintain a database.

Database Normalization Guidelines

Database normalization is the process of structuring a database in accordance with ***normal forms***- guidelines established to reduce data redundancy, while increasing data integrity in database design. While there are other forms, most database designers find it is adequate to design their relational databases to satisfy the normalization guidelines through the third or fourth normal "forms."

First normal form requires atomic, or unique, values at each column and row intersection in the entity table. There should be no repeating groups. Thus, no "Item1," "Item2" column design like you may see in a 'flat-file' table layout.

Second normal form requires that every "non-key" column in a table must depend on the primary key. A table must also not contain a "non-key" column that pertains to only part of a composite, or multi-column, primary key.

Third normal form requires that no "non-key" column should depend on another "non-key" column. This is very similar to the second normal form. You shouldn't have a field that is an attribute of a non-primary key column in a table.

Fourth normal form forbids independent "1-to-many" relationships between primary key columns and non-key columns.

SQL Variations and Core SQL

The specific implementation of the SQL language may vary by vendor within database management software. SQL was designed as a standardized language to implement basic functionality within these programs- including running queries on data, modifying data within tables, displaying views of data, and creating and modifying database structures and data access. Most vendors have included their own vendor-specific extensions to the SQL language. Therefore, you may encounter vendor-specific variations to the standard SQL, often with their own names, such as the "Transact-SQL" which is used within Microsoft SQL Server. The "core" SQL, is supported by all of the major database management systems, regardless of their own specific implementations and extensions.

Guide Conventions and Categories

This guide will refer to the core SQL within its examples. Most RDBMS Server and Microsoft Access, require a semicolon at the end of executabl examples of core SQL shown in this guide ***will not*** show a semicolon at t demonstrating core SQL and are not *literal examples* of SQL for any specific RDBMS. This guide will focus on the statements within standard SQL, grouped into four categories. **Data Definition Language (DDL)** statements, such as CREATE and ALTER, are used to create the database container, tables, and other objects. **Data Manipulation Language (DML)** statements, such as SELECT and INSERT, are used to manage the data contained within the tables. **Data Control Language (DCL)** statements, such as GRANT and REVOKE, are used to determine who can access the data and to set referential integrity. **Transactional Control Language (TCL)** statements, such as COMMIT and ROLLBACK, manage the transactions that occur within a database. The following notations are used in the syntax descriptions in the examples within this guide.

Notation	Example	Meaning
ALL CAPS	SELECT	The actual SQL code. Type this text exactly as shown.
Italics	*table_name*	SQL parameters to replace with content described by the italicized term.
|	ASC | DESC	Separates alternative choices from which to choose.
( )	(size)	Values to type for selected SQL commands. Include the parentheses when typing these values.
{ }	{ WHERE clause }	**Optional** or **RDBMS-depdendent** clauses or values. Do not type the braces.
[ ]	[* | *field1, field2*]	**Required** choices from which to select. Do not type the brackets.
etc.	*field1, field2, etc.*	Repeat the pattern established by the preceding values, as needed.

Data Definition Language (DDL)

Creating a Database

CREATE DATABASE *database_name*

Creating a Table

CREATE TABLE *table_name*
(
field_name1 data_type(size),
field_name2 data_type(size),
field_name3 data_type(size),
etc.
)

Creating an Index

Sort a table by values contained in one or more fields.

To create a standard index that allows duplicate field values:
CREATE INDEX *index_name*
ON *table_name (field_name)*

To create a unique index that does NOT allow for duplicates field values:
CREATE UNIQUE INDEX *index_name*
ON *table_name (field_name)*

Creating a User

CREATE USER *user_name*

Creating a Role

CREATE ROLE *role_name*

About SQL Constraints

A constraint is a limitation that is placed upon the allowable values within a field. Constraints can be added to CREATE TABLE or ALTER TABLE statements.

NOT NULL: Field will not accept NULL values.
UNIQUE: Ensures all values entered into the field are unique.
PRIMARY KEY: Defines a field (or combination of fields) within a table as being the primary key. Must be unique and cannot contain NULL values.
FOREIGN KEY: Ensures all values within the field correspond to values found within another table's PRIMARY KEY field. Used as a referential integrity check to ensure that records within a field have a corresponding value within a related table.
CHECK: Specifies the allowable values that can be entered into a table.
DEFAULT: Places a default value into the field specified when a record is entered.

Applying SQL Constraints

[CREATE | ALTER] TABLE *table_name*
(
field_name1 data_type(size) constraint_name,
field_name2 data_type(size) constraint_name,
field_name3 data_type(size) constraint_name,
etc.
)

Deleting Database Objects

To delete a database:
DROP DATABASE *database_name*

To delete a table within a database:
DROP TABLE *table_name*

To truncate a table within a database:
TRUNCATE TABLE *table_name*

To delete an index within a database:
DROP INDEX *index_name*

To delete an user within a database:
DROP USER *user_name*

To delete a role within a database:
DROP ROLE *role_name*

Modifying Table Structure

To alter a table to add a field:
ALTER TABLE *table_name*
ADD *field_name data_type*

To alter a table to delete a field:
ALTER TABLE *table_name*
DROP COLUMN *field_name*

To alter a table to modify a field's data type:
ALTER TABLE *table_name*
[MODIFY | ALTER] COLUMN *field_name data_type*

To alter a table to add an SQL constraint:
ALTER TABLE *table_name*
ADD { CONSTRAINT } *sql_constraint*

To alter a table to delete an SQL constraint:
ALTER TABLE *table_name*
DROP { CONSTRAINT } *sql_constraint*

TeachUcomp, Inc.
www.teachucomp.com
info@teachucomp.com
877.925.8080

General SQL Data Types

Data	Description
CHARACTER(N)	Fixed-length text, or character, string. N specifies the number of fixed characters in length that the field will contain.
VARCHAR(N) or CHARACTER VARYING(N)	Variable-length text, or character, string. N specifies the MAXIMUM number of characters that the field can contain.
BINARY(N)	Fixed-length binary string. N specifies the fixed length.
BOOLEAN	Stores a TRUE or FALSE value.
VARBINARY(N) or BINARY VARYING(N)	Variable-length binary string. N specifies the MAXIMUM length.
INTEGER(P)	Integer number values, with a precision of P.
SMALLINT	Integer number values with a precision of 5.
INTEGER	Integer number values with a precision of 10.
BIGINT	Integer number values with a precision of 19.
DECIMAL(P,S) or NUMERIC (P,S)	Stores an exact number with a precision of P and a scale of S. For example, a DECIMAL(9,2) would store a number that has 7 digits before the decimal point and 2 digits after the decimal point, with a total of 9 digits stored.
FLOAT(P)	Approximate-number data types for use with floating point numeric data. Floating point data is approximate; therefore, not all values in the data type range can be represented exactly. P is the number of bits used to store the mantissa of the float number in scientific notation and, therefore, dictates the precision and storage size.
REAL	Approximate-number data with a mantissa precision of 7.
FLOAT or DOUBLE PRECISION	Approximate-number data with a mantissa precision of 16.
DATE	Stores year, month, and day values.
TIME	Stores hour, minute, and second intervals.
TIMESTAMP	Stores year, month, day, hour, minute, and second intervals.
INTERVAL	Contains a number of integer fields, representing a period of time, depending on the type of interval.
ARRAY	A fixed-length, ordered set of elements.
MULTISET	A variable-length, unordered set of elements.
XML	Stores XML data.
MONEY, SMALLMONEY or CURRENCY	Stores a data type that represents monetary values. SMALLMONEY store a smaller ranges of values than MONEY. Not implemented in MySQL or Oracle RDBMS.

Data Manipulation Language (DML)

Inserting Records

INSERT INTO *table_name (field_name, field_name1, field_name2, etc.)*
VALUES (*value, value1, value2, etc.)*

Updating Records

UPDATE *table_name*
SET *field_name=update_value, field_name1=update_value1, etc.*
WHERE *field_name=existing_value*

Deleting Records

DELETE FROM *table_name*
WHERE *field_name=delete_value*

Selecting Records

To select specified fields from a table:
SELECT *field_name, field_name1, field_name2, etc.*
FROM *table_name*

To select specified fields from a table and only return unique record values:
SELECT DISTINCT *field_name, field_name1, field_name2, etc.*
FROM *table_name*

To select all fields from a table:
SELECT * FROM *table_name*

Selecting with the WHERE Clause

SELECT *field_name, field_name1, etc.*
FROM *table_name*
WHERE *field_name = criteria*

Sorting with the ORDER BY Clause

In order to sort in descending order, you must specify the DESC keyword after each named field.

SELECT *field_name, field_name1, etc.*
FROM *table_name*
WHERE *field_name = criteria*
ORDER BY *field_name* { ASC | DESC }, *field_name1* { ASC | DESC }, *etc.*

Grouping Records with the GROUP BY and Optional HAVING Clause

The optional HAVING clause determines which groups to display and can include aggregate functions.

SELECT *field_name, aggregate_function(field_name1), etc.*
FROM *table_name*
{ WHERE clause }
GROUP BY *field_name, etc.*
{ HAVING criteria }
{ ORDER BY field_name {ASC | DESC }, *etc.* }

Selecting from Multiple Tables with the JOIN Clause

Joins between two tables occur when the values within a PRIMARY KEY field of one table are linked to values within the FOREIGN KEY field of another table. Joins within the SELECT statement allow for access to data from multiple tables within a single result set. The different SQL joins are the INNER JOIN, the LEFT JOIN, the RIGHT JOIN, and the FULL JOIN.

SELECT *field_name, field_name1, field_name2, etc.*
FROM *table_name*
[INNER JOIN | LEFT JOIN | RIGHT JOIN | FULL JOIN]
table_name1
ON *table_name.primary_key = table_name1.foreign_key*

Combining Result Sets with UNION

The UNION operator combines the result sets of two or more SELECT statements into a single result set.

To create a UNION of two SELECT statements that returns only unique records values:
select_statement
UNION
select_statement1

To create a UNION of two SELECT statements that returns ALL records values within the statements:
select_statement
UNION ALL
select_statement1

Copying Records to a New Table

The SELECT INTO statement is used to copy the result set of a SELECT statement into a new table that is created by the SELECT INTO statement.

SELECT [* | *field_name, field_name1, etc.*]
INTO *new_table_name*
FROM *table_name*
WHERE *field_name = criteria*

Appending Records from One Table Into Another Existing Table

The INSERT INTO SELECT statement copies records from one table with a SELECT statement, and then appends them into another existing table.

INSERT INTO *table_name* (*field_name, field_name1, field_name2, etc.*)
SELECT [* | *field_name3, field_name4, etc.*]
FROM *table_name1*
WHERE *field_name3 = criteria*

Creating a Subquery

Nest a query within another query to create a subquery. Subqueries can be nested inside many types of DML statements, such as the standard SELECT statement, a SELECT INTO statement, an INSERT INTO statement, an UPDATE statement, and the DELETE statement. You can also nest subqueries within other subqueries. Subqueries are placed within parentheses inside of the main statement.

primary_query
(
SELECT [* | *field_name, field_name1, etc.*]
FROM *table_name*
{ WHERE clause }
{ GROUP BY *field_name, etc.* }
{ HAVING *criteria* }
{ ORDER BY *field_name* { ASC | *DESC* }, *etc.* }
)
primary_query

Common Comparison Operators Used in the WHERE Clause

Data	Description
=	Equals. Used to find values that are equal to a value that you specify.
<> or !=	Not equal to. Used to select values that are NOT equal to a value you specify. The symbol used can change depending on the version of SQL implemented within your RDBMS.
>	Greater than. Used to find values that are greater than a value specified.
<	Less than. Used to find values that are less than a value specified.
> =	Greater than or equal to. Used to find values that are greater than or equal to a value specified.
< =	Less than or equal to. Used to find values that are less than or equal to a value specified.
BETWEEN	Used to find values including and between two values that are specified.
LIKE	Used to find values that match a pattern that is specified.
IN	Used to find values that match multiple values within a list of values that are specified.
AND	Used to join multiple selection criteria together. Selects records that match both criteria joined by the AND operator.
OR	Used to join multiple selection criteria. Selects records that match either criteria joined together by the OR operator.

Common Notations Used for Literal Values and Wildcard Characters

Notation	Use
' ' or " "	Specifies a text value or text string. Sometimes used to denote any non-numeric value.
None	Numeric values do not use any notation. Numbers are signified by a lack of notation.
# #	Specifies a date/time value in Microsoft Access.
[ ]	Specifies a parameter or other field name value to use as the criteria in Microsoft Access. Example: [table.field]. Used to denote a set of initial characters to match when used in conjunction with wildcard characters in most other RDBMS. Example: '[a-d]%'
% or *	Wildcard character. Used to denote multiple unknown characters.
_ or ?	Wildcard character. Used to denote a single unknown character.

Data Control Language (DCL)

About Data Control Language

Data Control Language (DCL) is used within SQL to grant or deny privileges, which are permissions to perform specific tasks within a database, to users. Not every RDBMS will fully implement DCL within their SQL. Other database programs, like Microsoft Access, use a separate security mechanism to determine user access and privileges not tied to SQL. Consult your RDBMS documentation to find out the level of DCL implementation that exists. DCL statements are used by the database administrator, or owner, to grant or revoke privileges to and from users and roles. **To create or delete users or roles, refer to the *Data Definition Language* section of this guide, as those statements create and delete database objects.**

Granting User or Role Privileges

The GRANT statement is a DCL statement used by the database administrator or owner to grant privileges to other database users and roles.

GRANT *privilege*
ON *db_object*
TO [*user_name* | *role_name* | PUBLIC]
{ WITH GRANT OPTION }

Revoking User or Role Privileges

The REVOKE statement is used to revoke privileges from database users and roles. Check your RDBMS documentation to see if the REVOKE statement, when used in conjunction with the PUBLIC clause, will also revoke the privilege from the object owner or database administrator. If so, you may need to specify the owner's name in several specific GRANT statements following a general REVOKE. Use caution when using the PUBLIC clause with the REVOKE statement. Check how a PUBLIC clause within a GRANT or REVOKE statement interacts with individually specified GRANT and REVOKE statements that were previously issued.

REVOKE *privilege*
ON *db_object*
FROM [*user_name* | *role_name* | PUBLIC]

About Privileges

Privileges provide various levels of permission to create, edit, and delete database objects. The exact types of permissions that can be granted will vary depending upon the relational database management system that you are using. You must check your specific RDBMS documentation to be sure which privileges are available. The following table lists commonly used privileges that will often be implemented within relational database management systems that support DCL statements.

Commonly Used Privileges

Privilege	Description
CREATE	Allows users to create objects. Often cited as CREATE db_object, where the "db_object" parameter is the type of database object that the privilege allows them to create. Also cited as CREATE ALL to allow the user to create any type of database object.
ALTER	Allows users to alter objects. Often cited as ALTER db_object, where the "db_object" parameter is the type of database object that the privilege allows them to alter. Also cited as ALTER ALL to allow the user to alter any type of database object.
DROP	Allows users to delete objects. Often cited as DROP db_object, where the "db_object" parameter is the type of database object that the privilege allows them to delete. Also cited as DROP ALL to allow the user to delete any type of database object.
INSERT	Allows the user to insert records into a table.
UPDATE	Allows the user to update records within a table.
DELETE	Allows the user to delete records within a table.
SELECT	Allows the user to select records within a table.
EXECUTE	Allows the user to execute a stored procedure or function

Altering Users

Use the ALTER USER statement to alter information about a user, which may include the user's database password, schema or database access, and login information. Note that this statement is technically classified as Data Definition Language (DDL), as it defines the objects within the database. Note that the WITH clause is shown within braces as it is not universally applied amongst RDBMS implementations.

ALTER USER *user_name*
{ WITH } *alterations*

Altering Roles

Use the ALTER ROLE statement to alter existing roles within your RDBMS to add and remove users from being associated with that role, to rename a role, or to change other attributes of the role in some way. Note that this statement is technically classified as Data Definition Language (DDL), as it defines the objects within the database. Note that the WITH clause is shown within braces as it is not universally applied amongst RDBMS implementations.

ALTER ROLE *role_name*
{ WITH } *alterations*

Transaction Control Language (TCL)

About Transaction Control Language

Transaction Control Language (TCL) statements within SQL are the statements used to control a set of Data Manipulation Language (DML) statements that are executed as a single unit called a *transaction*. TCL ensures that either all the changes made by the DML statements within the transaction are committed to the database or none of them are. While many of the major commands within TCL are fairly standard, there is quite a bit of variation in the execution of the transactions within each RDBMS. Check your RDBMS documentation to see what options are available for transactions within your system.

The TRANSACTION Statement

The BEGIN TRANSACTION or START TRANSACTION statement is used to initiate a transaction within an RDBMS. If the transaction statements that follow fail to execute, then the changes that were made by the statements can be set back to this point. The exact command used to initiate a transaction will vary by RDBMS, but is most commonly either BEGIN TRANSACTION or START TRANSACTION. The core SQL of this statement is shown below. Note that the "work" parameter represents the SQL statements that will be executed within the transaction. The COMMIT statement is used after the work has been completed to commit those changes to the database. The ROLLBACK statement is used to undo any changes to the database caused by the work back to the point at which the TRANSACTION statement was initiated.

[BEGIN | START] TRANSACTION
work
[COMMIT | ROLLBACK]

SQL Functions and Aliases

About SQL Functions

A function is a computation that is executed by invoking a single-word command that returns a value. While some functions, such as SUM, are universally accepted by all RDBMS, there are also variations of function names between RDBMS. For example, while almost all RDBMS can provide you with the current date in a function, the name of the function used to accomplish that is SYSDATE within MySQL and Oracle, while it is named GETDATE within SQL Server and DATE within Access. Check the documentation of your specific RDBMS to know which function names are available to use.

Functions are classified as being either deterministic or non-deterministic. A deterministic function will always return the same result whenever it is used with the same set of inputs. A non-deterministic function may return a different result when used with the same set of inputs. For example, the SUM function is a deterministic function, as it will always return the same result if given the same input parameters or variables. In contrast, the SYSDATE or GETDATE functions, which are used to retrieve the current date in MySQL or SQL Server, are non-deterministic functions as they will return a different answer when used.

Aggregate functions perform a summarizing operation upon a group of values or inputs to return a summary value. Scalar functions are performed upon a single value and return a single value. For example, the SUM function is used to create a summary value from selected values within a field. However the LOWER function (called LCASE in Microsoft Access), will simply return a single field value in all lowercase characters.

Common Aggregate Functions

Function	Description
AVG()	Calculates the average value of a column of numeric type. Returns the average of all non NULL values
COUNT()	Returns the number of rows in a table satisfying the criteria specified in the WHERE clause. Sets the number of rows or non NULL column values.*
MAX()	Used to find the maximum value or highest value of a certain column or expression. Useful to determine the largest of all selected values of a column.
MIN()	Used to find the minimum value or lowest value of a column or expression. Useful to determine the smallest of all selected values of a column.
SUM()	Returns the sum of all or distinct values in a set.

*Except for the COUNT() function, SQL aggregate functions ignore null. Because an aggregate function operates on a set of values, it is often used with the GROUP BY clause of the SELECT statement. The GROUP BY clause divides the result set into groups of values and the aggregate function returns a single value for each group. Aggregate functions as expressions can only be used in the select list of a SELECT statement, either a subquery or an outer query, or a HAVING clause.

Calculated Fields and Column Aliases

You can use scalar functions within SQL to create calculated fields within SELECT statements. This allows you to display the result of a calculation within a field in the result set of a query. The calculation can refer to columns within the tables selected in the FROM clause of the SELECT statement. You may want to give the calculated field, also called a "calculated column," its own name so that the user will not see the calculated expression as the field name within the result set. You can change the displayed title of any field within a result set, calculated or not, by using a column alias. While calculated fields are most often given column aliases, you can apply an alias to any field in the result set. For example, assume that you are selecting a "QuantitySold" field and a "UnitPrice" field from a "Sales" table. You want the result set of the query to display these two columns with spaces within their names and you also want a third column to display the result of multiplying the values within the "QuantitySold" and "UnitPrice" columns for each record. You want the third calculated field in the result set to have the display name of "Sales Subtotal." The AS keyword is used to apply an alias to a field within the statement. You could create a simple query that would contain the following SQL. *Example*:

SELECT QuantitySold AS 'Quantity Sold', UnitPrice AS 'Unit Price', QuantitySold * UnitPrice AS 'Sales Subtotal'
FROM Sales

When creating the calculated field, enter the calculation to perform within the field listing of the SELECT clause within the SELECT statement. To use a column alias, follow the calculation or field name with the AS keyword, and then the name of the column alias within either single or double quotation marks per your RDBMS specifications.

SELECT *field_name, field_name1, etc., calculated_field* AS '*alias_name*', *etc.*
FROM *table_name*

Table Aliases

You can use table aliases in SQL to make referencing table names within complex SQL statements easier. For example, if you have a "CustomerID" field within a "Customers" table and also have a "CustomerID" field within a "Sales" table, you must use the dot notation reference of table_name.field_name for the "CustomerID" field within the SQL statement so that the database will know which "CustomerID" field you are referencing within the SQL statement. To simplify the SQL statement, you can apply an alias to a table name to simplify the table_name.field_name expressions. The core SQL used to create a table alias within the FROM clause of the SELECT statement is shown below. The "*field_name*" parameter is the name of a field within a table referred to within the FROM clause. The "*table_name*" parameter is the name of a table within the database. The "*alias_name*" parameter is the alias name that you want to give to the table.

SELECT *alias_name.field_name, alias_name.field_name1, alias_name, etc.*
FROM *table_name* AS *alias_name*

Views

About Views

A view is a virtual table that is based on the results of a SELECT statement. Similar to the result set of a query, they display the most recent data from the underlying tables from which they are constructed. A view will often present data from joined base tables in a relational database, in a more user-friendly format. It is also possible to query a view by using the name of the view within the FROM clause of the SELECT statement.

Creating a View

Use the CREATE VIEW statement to create a view of the data within your base tables as a separate virtual table within your database. The core SQL of the CREATE VIEW statement is shown below. The "*view_name*" parameter is the name of the new view, and the "*select_statement*" parameter is the SELECT statement used to define which records and fields that will appear within the view.

CREATE VIEW *view_name* AS
select_statement

Altering a View

Use the ALTER VIEW statement to redefine the display of data within a named view. The core SQL of the ALTER VIEW statement is shown below. The "*view_name*" parameter is the name of the view to edit and the "*select_statement*" parameter is the SELECT statement used to define which records and fields will appear within the edited view.

ALTER VIEW *view_name* AS
select_statement

Removing a View

Use the DROP VIEW statement to remove a named view from a database. The core SQL of the DROP VIEW statement is shown below. The "*view_name*" parameter is the name of the view to delete.

DROP VIEW *view_name*

ISBN 978-1-941854-73-0
9 781941 854730

Made in the USA